The Flipchart Guide™ to

Customer
Advisory
Boards

Volume 2

How to execute a world-class CAB meeting

An operations manual for CAB managers

J. Michael Gospe, Jr.

Author of *The Marketing High Ground*

The Flipchart Guide™ *to Customer Advisory Boards*

Why flipcharts? A tool of choice for many facilitators is the flipchart. While this may seem old-school in an era of modern technology, the flipchart visual brings everyone together. It offers a shared experience where all participants can see, comment on, and benefit from the key points, creative thoughts, and "aha!" moments captured from the conversation in real time. It's a customer-engaging technique that encourages the discussion to grow in a purposeful direction.

Two volumes of the *Flipchart Guide*™ *to Customer Advisory Boards* lead you and your team through every step of the CAB process, showing you how to define and set up the right types of customer conversations that will unlock the Rosetta Stone of customer understanding. They offer strategies, agendas, and case studies used by companies that have successfully deployed CABs to enhance their relationships with strategic customers, improve customer loyalty, and sustain a competitive advantage.

Volume 1: Is your company ready?
Written for executive leaders, this guidebook explores CAB strategies and helps readers assess their organizational, operational, and cultural readiness for embracing a CAB.

- Discover if a CAB is appropriate for your company.
- See how executives use CABs to tune their company's strategic direction.
- Learn where CABs fit into the overall "voice of the customer" (VOC) model.
- Study the *Top 10 List* of what all executives need to know about CABs.

iii

Volume 2: How to execute a world-class CAB meeting
Written for CAB managers, this guidebook provides an operations manual for success:

- View the master timeline for producing successful CAB meetings.
- Unlock the criteria for determining which customers to invite and how to invite them.
- Discover how to build an agenda that will engage customers.
- Review tips and tricks for working cross-organizationally to prepare effective content and presentations.
- Know what to expect from a facilitator.
- Learn how to share CAB feedback internally so your organization can take action.

For more articles and information about CABs, please visit **http://customeradvisoryboards.wordpress.com**.

Also by J. Michael Gospe, Jr.

Marketing Campaign Development: *What marketing executives need to know about architecting global integrated marketing campaigns*

The Marketing High Ground: *The essential playbook for B2B marketing practitioners everywhere*

The Marketing High Ground series
- **Personas:** *A guidebook on how to build a persona*
- **Positioning Statements:** *A guidebook on how to build, critique, and defend a positioning statement*
- **The Message Box:** *A guidebook on how to tell your story with customer-ready messaging*
- **The Role of the Campaign Manager:** *A primer for driving integrated marketing plans*

Websites
- *Marketing Campaign Development*
  http://marketingcampaigndevelopment.wordpress.com

- *The Marketing High Ground*
  http://marketinghighground.wordpress.com

To Allison, Sean, Tina
and all first-time CAB managers
- May this guidebook
speed you on your way to success

Acknowledgement

Thank you, to all the wonderful people who have generously shared their customer advisory board stories and best practices with me over the past ten years, especially those who have provided me with such expert coaching on this book: Tina Brown, Andrea Davidowitz, Diane Demeester, Sharon Durham, Brian Gentile, Catherine Gibson, Diane Kauffman McGary, Anne Merkert, Sridhar Ramanathan, Susan Thomas, Jeff Tinker, and Melissa Zieger.

I am grateful, too, for the gentle editing from my editors, both of whom are KickStart Alliance co-founders and partners, Mary Gospe and Mary Sullivan. My deep appreciation also goes out to Joe Bednarski for his exceptional work on the cover and figures used in this book.

And most importantly, thank you to my clients, collaborators, and co-conspirators that I have had the honor of working with. Together, we've journeyed to the marketing high ground.

Other types of advisory boards

This book is about customer advisory boards (CABs), sometimes referred to as customer advisory councils (CACs) or executive advisory boards (EABs). But there are also additional types of advisory boards available to business-to-business (B2B) companies, and each serve a unique purpose. These include partner advisory boards (PABs), technology advisory boards (TABs), and influencer advisory boards (IABs).

Companies that sell primarily through distribution channels may be interested in sponsoring a PAB in an effort to improve partner relations and help partners accelerate sales. Companies on the forefront of innovation may be interested in sponsoring a TAB made up of scientists and technologists from the research and development community. The IAB is a new breed, focusing not on the traditional influencers of analysts and journalists, but on individuals whose leadership, innovation, and social interactions inspire others to think differently in how they use technologies, products, and applications.

Although the practical operations of all advisory boards are run in a similar fashion (e.g. facilitated face-to-face meetings held once or twice a year with a carefully selected small group of leaders), there are important differences including the invitee list, specific meeting objectives, and the relevant agendas. Nuances of PABs, TABs, and IABs are not covered in this book; however, the general best practices for establishing an advisory board initiative shared in these pages can be applied to them equally well.

CONTENTS

INTRODUCTION

I was introduced to my first customer advisory board (CAB) project in early 2002. An enterprise chief marketing officer told me he had a problem. His CAB meeting was scheduled to take place in two months and he needed someone to run it. Could I help? Truth be told, until this point I had never heard of a CAB. Sure, I knew what each of those three words meant individually, but connecting them in this way was a new concept.

I looked for books on the topic and casually interviewed a few of my colleagues. Alas, I found no templates or advice to guide me or set my expectations. I took the assignment with a healthy dose of excitement and uncertainty, trusting my instincts that I'd be able to figure it out. Through that project I learned that in addition to common sense, managing a CAB meeting required organizational diplomacy and operational finesse because of the strategic nature of the meeting's objective and agenda. There were some bumps along the way, but the end result proved to be a very successful meeting between company executives and an elite group of customer decision makers. So much so that I was allowed the privilege of guiding eight more CAB meetings over the next four years for this company in the US and

1

Europe. And this success caught the attention of other companies curious about CABs. I quickly found an awakening of companies, big and small, looking for best practices to engage customers in a new type of conversation about strategies and business directions. These companies were the early adopters of what today has become a standard approach to CABs.

Since 2002 I've been working with companies of all sizes to customize and facilitate their CAB meetings. And I've learned a lot. I've learned that a successful CAB meeting requires alignment and agreement among company executives who not only are eager and willing to listen to their customers, but who are committed to take action based on the input and feedback they collect. I've also learned that effective CAB meetings don't just happen; they require careful planning so that the right customer executives from the right companies are invited to answer the right questions at the right time. And I've learned that taking short-cuts, however tempting, (like allowing the sales team to dictate the invitation list or waiting until a week before the meeting to finalize the agenda), creates problems that can easily been avoided.

What is a CAB?

A CAB is a strategy-level focus group – a sounding board for your leadership team to learn from and better understand your most strategic customers. This representative group of eight to 16 customers meets in person once or twice a year to offer advice and perspective on your company direction, value proposition, and product suite. During CAB meetings, these customers interact with your company's senior staff who have the authority and responsibility to act on the information gathered. They may also interact with you, and with each other, via webinars or through email correspondence throughout the year.

In its most effective implementation, a CAB is a cross-functional *initiative*, not an event, and not a single meeting held once or in isolation from the rest of your marketing activities. CAB meetings are unlike any other meeting you will run. They are not sales meetings, nor are they user group sessions offering tutorials or examining product feature details. And, they are not impromptu customer appreciation events where you play golf and socialize. All of those types of interactions are incredibly important and each play a role in the relationship you nurture with your customers. But these are not CABs. It's important to understand the distinction.

Executing a world-class CAB initiative requires an unwavering focus on understanding the needs of customers as well as they themselves do. Equally important is the tight alignment that must exist across the company to ensure execution of a focused business plan and product roadmap based, in part, on this very relevant customer input. Unfortunately, the business landscape is littered with companies who refused to take the time to listen to their customers. They thought they didn't need to. The act of listening begins by asking relevant questions of the appropriate leaders in your customer base. But this is just the tip of the iceberg when it comes to the information you need in order to grow your business. Consider that what your customers say they want from you is probably no different from what they tell your competitors. So, what's the point? Where are the opportunities for product differentiation?

The most visionary corporate leaders are the ones who not only hear the words spoken by their customers but also read the unspoken needs that lay just below the surface. This type of listening fuels intuition. It's the key to what separates the most innovative companies from a sea of competitors who all have access to the same data but struggle to understand the meaning.

The benefit of customer insight comes from reaching a level of true comprehension of how your customers think as well as behave. And for that, it's critically important to know what questions to ask, and how and when to ask them. For example, all customers want to be pleasantly surprised and delighted, yet it would be counterproductive to ask them directly, *"What can we do to surprise and delight you?"* Either they would respond with superficial, off-the-cuff requests or they wouldn't know how to answer the question. So, you need to find other questions that will provide the level of insight and perspective you need to truly understand the customer. And that requires some finesse.

This book is the CAB meeting operations manual I wish I had ten years ago. If you are a first time CAB manager or CAB sponsor, this book is for you.

Helping me develop content for both **Volume 1** and **Volume 2** and share it in a way that is (hopefully) both engaging and practical are customer engagement experts who I am honored to know. Customer advocates from Aspect, AT&T, Citrix, HP, Oracle, NFI, Rackspace, Siemens, Wells Fargo, and many others working at start-ups and enterprise companies have helped me bring these best practices to life. And I offer them to you.

Four CAB objectives

There are four primary objectives for a well-run CAB meeting. A company may want to achieve just one, all four, or a combination of these general objectives. To:

1. **Gain a better understanding of the trends, drivers, and priorities shaping your customers' businesses**, and to explore how your company can become a more valuable partner in light of these influences.

2. **Validate your company's value proposition and strategic direction**, ensuring your business is in sync with your customers' needs and expectations.

3. **Review, assess, or brainstorm product direction and opportunities,** improving solutions, interaction, and customer satisfaction.

4. **Collaborate on shared business issues**, thereby strengthening the relationship between your executives and customer decision makers, and fostering peer-to-peer networking opportunities between your customers.

If the above objectives mesh with your interests, then a CAB is the right initiative for you. This is a critical first step because CABs are often misunderstood as having other objectives that are *not appropriate*. For example:

x   Do not use the CAB as a sales event to drive immediate bookings. *Instead, host a breakfast meeting for a mix of customers and prospects where customers are invited to talk about specific applications and use cases for your products and services.* (This is worth repeating: **the CAB is not a sales event!** If you attempt to sell to customers during this meeting, they will feel that you tricked them, your brand image will suffer, and they will not return to future CAB meetings.)

x   Do not use the CAB merely to socialize with customers. *Instead, add a customer-appreciation day at the end of your annual user conference.*

x   Do not use the CAB to prioritize product features or conduct product training. *Instead, hold a product focus group or training event with actual users.* (Decision-makers attend CABs; they may or may not be the actual users of your products or services.)

x   Do not use any CAB meeting to publicly launch new products or services. *Instead, execute an integrated marketing campaign to introduce new products and services, taking full advantage of relevant and timely marketing and social media vehicles necessary to engage prospects and customers through their buying cycle.*

x   Do not use the CAB to discuss support issues unique to each customer. *Instead, set up a private quarterly (or semi-annual or annual) account review meeting with each customer.*

Why your customers will participate in a CAB

Senior decision makers attend CAB meetings for three primary reasons. First, they rarely have the opportunity to network with their peers to discuss and debate how the world around them affects their business. They are eager to explore and compare notes with other executives who are wrestling with the same business challenges. They want to learn from each other.

Second, they want to get a clear picture of your vision and business strategy and explore how they can influence it and take greater advantage of the benefits your company offers. Briefings on product roadmaps, early access to products before general release, hands-on with prototypes, and unprecedented access to your company's leadership team all provide a unique and compelling opportunity to gather and discuss information that can only be obtained under a non-disclosure agreement.

And third, it is very rare to find vendors that are genuinely interested in learning what their customers think. Customers have opinions they want to share with their vendors, if only the vendors would ask them sincerely, politely, and with an honest intention to listen and act on their input. So, when a company extends a thoughtful invitation to senior decision makers to come together with their peers and provide guidance and feedback, many customer executives jump at the chance. To confirm these reasons, here is a selection of feedback customers have offered at the close of CAB meetings.

"I feel honored to be invited to participate with this elite group of strategic customers."

"It's about time! I've been waiting for a meeting like this where I can share feedback. Thank you for inviting me."

"I appreciate your spending time on the strategic issues that are important to my business."

"It's not often that I am invited to contribute in an executive roundtable. I very much appreciated the opportunity to offer my input and feedback on your company vision and direction."

"I enjoyed participating in a lot of very interesting discussions and spending time together and exchanging ideas."

CAB roles and responsibilities

When it comes to executing a world-class CAB initiative, there are six key roles:

- *Customer members:* While under a non-disclosure agreement, CAB members attend meetings with the expectation of sharing open and honest feedback in a constructive manner with your executive team. The typical length of membership is between 12 to 18 months and includes participating in one or two face-to-face meetings per year, in addition to other forms of engagement throughout the year. Membership is non-binding, meaning that there are neither legal requirements nor compensation offered for their participation.

- *Executive leader (CXO, VP, or Business Unit General Manager):* While your executive leader will not be involved in the operational details of planning the CAB, he or she must maintain a visible presence and personal interest in the CAB as being a powerful asset to the company. The leader is an advocate for the CAB and looks for opportunities to rally and encourage the team doing the work. There is no substitute for attention provided by the executive leader. His or her involvement shows the importance of the CAB. Without it, employees will be reluctant to engage.

- *CAB sponsor (frequently the CMO or VP of marketing):* The job of the CAB sponsor is to remove any internal obstacles that may derail the successful execution of the initiative. When internal politics get in the way, or there is a lack of cross-functional participation, the CAB sponsor steps in to align operational priorities and ensures the CAB is treated as a strategic priority and not a special project where people participate "as a favor" if and when they have the time. The CAB sponsor will also track recommendations and assign action items that result from the CAB meetings.

- *CAB manager* (*may be a VP or director of marketing, product management, customer experience, or strategic planning*): The CAB manager owns the planning and execution of the CAB meeting. As master program manager, he or she oversees everything from the selection of customers to invite, to working with content owners on the formation of the agenda, to engaging the facilitator (internal or external), to coordinating the actual CAB meeting, to documenting the meeting, and to guiding the follow-up engagement with customers. Planning a successful CAB takes an average 12 weeks of preparation, and the CAB manager drives this process.

- *Logistics coordinator* (*usually the events manager*): This individual is responsible for all the logistical details for any CAB meeting, including managing the contract with the meeting hall or hotel, coordinating travel with customers, developing the welcome kit, and answering questions from customers regarding their attendance.

- *Facilitator:* The facilitator may be an internal resource or an external CAB-facilitation expert. If you choose to hire a professional CAB facilitator to guide your meeting, he or she will be involved in every step of the planning process. The professional facilitator will offer you and your content team guidance, templates, and a methodology for developing the most effective agenda, presentations, and discussion modules designed to meet your specific CAB objectives. While the role of the facilitator can be held by an internal resource, keep in mind that the art of facilitation is a skill that he or she may want to polish before the meeting. Ask if your internal facilitator would like assistance preparing for their role. This step can help them deal with nervousness, or practice engagement techniques that will not drive the discussion in a consciously- or unconsciously-biased way. Also watch out for conflicting priorities that may become distractions that will limit his or her involvement. If duties require your internal facilitator to be elsewhere and he or she can't personally commit the time required to prepare for or to be 100% certain of his or her availability to attend the CAB meeting, do your company a favor and hire a professional CAB facilitator.

Bringing your CAB to life

With your CAB objectives confirmed and the executive staff aligned, you're ready for the next step. The most customer-engaging, rewarding CAB meetings follow a set of operational best-practices that keep the attention on the customer, their priorities, and the opportunities for your company to help them succeed.

We'll tackle the next steps together.

1: COUNTDOWN TO A CAB

On average, it takes 12 weeks to plan a CAB because of the things you cannot control: your customers' schedules and the availability of your executive staff and discussion-topic owners to prepare for the CAB meeting. Chances are that the schedules of the executives you want to invite are already booked 60 days in advance. In addition, the topic owners in your company have many priorities competing for their time. While planning discussion modules and presentations are not difficult tasks, they do take time. And, in reality, the CAB is just another assignment they need to fit into their already busy schedules.

Avoid scrambling to pull CAB materials together at the last minute. Otherwise the quality of the engagement suffers. Customers will know when you haven't thought through the material. You need a timeline that allows you to balance the CAB preparation process with both structure and flexibility. Figure 1 offers a high-level master timeline that encompasses five key areas of activity.

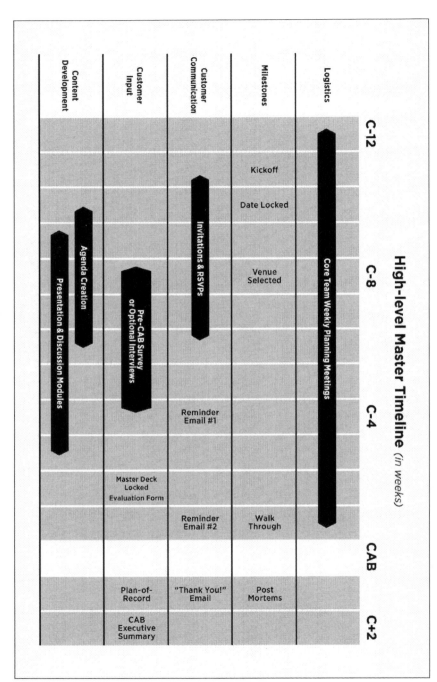

Figure 1: This master timeline for planning a CAB meeting.

While many of the elements overlap, it's easier to understand the master timeline if we dissect it as follows:

1. Logistics
2. Milestones
3. Customer communication
4. Customer input
5. Content development

1. Logistics

Determining who is on the CAB core team is the first step. A small core group drives the CAB preparation process and usually consists of the CAB manager, logistics coordinator(s), and the facilitator. (First-time CAB managers may find value in hiring an external professional CAB facilitator to guide them through the entire preparation process. See chapter 7 for more details.) This group establishes a cadence of weekly meetings to drive a highly productive and informative CAB preparation process. These meetings start as early as twelve weeks before the CAB (C-12) and run right up to the week of the CAB meeting.

An extended team consisting of other stakeholders and content experts will participate in milestone meetings, as they will contribute to setting the agenda and finalizing presentations and discussion topics. Regardless, the core team is tasked with driving the timeline, managing the milestones, gently guiding the content owners and executives to meet deadlines, and communicating internally the status of all CAB preparations.

The first core team meeting is focused on setting operational expectations, agreeing upon templates to track their progress, and developing the master schedule. Careful attention must be placed on selecting a date for the CAB meeting that works for the executive team and customer attendees.

In the following weeks the core team coordinates the following:

- Setting the date for the CAB meeting
- Selecting customers to invite (chapter 2)
- Overseeing the invitation process (chapter 3)
- Evaluating hotel or conference locations and venues (chapter 4)
- Guiding agenda creation (chapter 5)
- Driving the development of presentation content and discussion modules (chapter 6).

And finally, after the CAB meeting concludes, the core team will regroup to conduct a post-mortem to evaluate its success and consider changes for the next CAB meeting.

2. Milestones

Of the many steps that trigger a variety of action items during the CAB preparation process, the most important are the ones that set expectations. These are the following:

- The kickoff meeting (held in week C-11)
- Locking in the date for the CAB meeting (typically set in week C-10)
- Selecting the venue (ideally no later than week C-8)
- Conducting the executive CAB meeting dry-run (usually in C-1)
- Conducting the post mortem review meetings (advisably before week C+2)

Let's consider them one at a time.

The **kickoff meeting** (held in week C-11) marks the beginning of the *official* CAB preparation process because it is visible to the organization and it is the first time the extended team will be engaged. The objective of the kickoff meeting is simple: *To launch the CAB initiative, determine next steps, and assign owners.* The CAB manager or CAB sponsor runs this meeting. In addition to the CAB core team, attendees include the appropriate members of the executive staff, key stakeholders, and topic contributors who will help identify which customers to invite, determine the agenda, and produce the final presentation materials. Here's a typical agenda for a 60-minute kickoff meeting:

1. *Introduce the CAB initiative (5 minutes):* The CAB sponsor or CAB manager defines the CAB and explains the reasons how and why it fits within the company's priorities today. He or she will also explain the desired outcome from this kickoff meeting, namely, to develop a rough agenda and assign owners to help refine the agenda and discussion topics in the weeks that follow.

2. *Define the CAB objectives (20 minutes)*: Review the specific objectives for the upcoming CAB meeting. This is an opportunity to share examples of what a CAB meeting looks like, setting expectations for the type of content and interaction appropriate for discussion with these strategic customers. Also, set expectations regarding the outcome and how data gathered from the meeting will be used internally. This overview is especially helpful for team members who have never before participated in a CAB. (For additional information regarding CAB objectives and

case studies, please refer to *The Flipchart Guide™ to Customer Advisory Boards, Volume 1: Is your company ready?*)

3. *Interactive discussion (25 minutes):* This is the first of several brainstorming sessions you will conduct with team members regarding possible CAB discussion topics. Appropriate lead-off questions include: "Where do we need customer input and feedback regarding our roadmaps and strategies? What questions are we most interested in asking customers? What can we learn from our customers?" Answers to these questions will guide the development of a customer-engaging agenda that is very relevant to your company.

4. *Next steps (10 minutes):* This meeting is a prelude to the detailed planning work that will unfold in the coming weeks. With that in mind, the final piece of the kickoff meeting is the presentation of a master timeline and the assignment of topic owners. Subject-matter experts will work together to tune and finalize the agenda and build the appropriate content for the presentations.

Setting a date for the CAB meeting (typically by week C-10) is a critical decision point, and it starts with confirming the availability of your leadership team. Because schedules are tricky to coordinate, it's best to understand your executives' schedules before setting expectations with customers regarding the proposed date of the CAB meeting. The earlier you can lock this on the executive calendar, the better. Once set, you can test the date in the CAB invitation email (see chapter 3). If enough customers indicate the date works for them, you can officially lock the date and begin working on the other details. If, however, most customers are not able to attend, you have time to revisit other options with the executive team.

Venue selection (ideally no later than week C-8) is also a critical decision point because customers will be eager to solidify their travel plans. Watch out for competing conferences that may overlap with your CAB meeting target date. You have more negotiating power and flexibility with hotels and conference venues if you can lock this in early.

The executive walk-thru (usually in week C-1), other than the kickoff meeting, is likely the only time you will have all the attending executives in the room at the same time. This meeting is very important because it is your chance to clarify expectations regarding the meeting and the appropriate rules of engagement. This is typically a one-hour meeting that includes the following:

- Reviewing the list of the attending customers
- Sharing the final agenda
- Explaining how the meeting will be facilitated
- Providing details regarding the networking reception and dinner
- Answering questions regarding the meeting, logistics, and rules of engagement

The post-mortem review meetings (conducted by week C+2) should not be overlooked. They can provide a wealth of information. Two meetings that will benefit your company are:

1. Core-team post-mortem meeting – Review all aspects of the CAB meeting including the quality of the venue, hotel accommodations, networking reception, customer communications process, and the CAB preparation process as a whole.

2. Executive review meeting – All attending executives regroup to reflect on the feedback and guidance provided by CAB customers. They can also agree upon action items including how they will share this feedback internally.

Sometimes the attending executives schedule a one-hour executive debrief immediately after the last customer departs. One CAB manager reflected, "This was invaluable to have the company execs spend some time verbalizing what they heard, agreeing and disagreeing with each other, and assigning action items on the spot while the information was still incredibly fresh. Their feedback and synthesis made the reporting process much easier, more accurate, and increased the effectiveness of the CAB session tenfold." This is a great way for them to compare notes before being confronted by the other priorities when they return to the office.

Other teams have a CAB review meeting as part of their next executive staff meeting, or they schedule a separate meeting just for this purpose. Because memories fade with time, have a review meeting within two weeks of the CAB meeting.

3. Customer communication

The secret to securing customer participation and setting their expectations about the meetings is in the membership invitation process (described in detail in chapter 3). Because of scheduling challenges, start the invitation process as early as possible (as early as C-11 weeks). Because the CAB is by invitation only and space is limited, the process starts by identifying a list of your top tier customers (refer to chapter 2) and inviting them first. To manage the limited capacity, invitations need to be staggered so you avoid the problem of having too many people accept the membership invitation. As a result, it may take as long as five or six weeks to confirm all customer seats are filled.

Sending a CAB membership invitation via email is acceptable. Hand-written invitations are not typical, although if that fits the style of your company, you may do so. Either way, a written invitation is not enough to ensure a response. To improve the odds of a positive response, assign an executive to each customer and have them follow-up with a personal call. The formation of a CAB implies that this elite, invitation-only group of strategic customers will enjoy a more intimate conversation with executive leaders. A good way to embody this intent is with your executives taking time out to make a personal connection. The email provides the reason for the executive to call; and customers will enjoy the personal attention from your leadership team.

Don't forget the importance of the reminder emails and the often-forgotten thank-you email that works best if it comes within 24 hours of the close of the meeting. Some executives go the extra mile to pen a handwritten thank-you letter, offering a nice personal touch.

4. Customer input

Whether this is your first or a later CAB meeting, it is customary to allow customers the opportunity to shape the agenda. Either a 20-minute personal interview conducted over the phone or a simple online survey is appropriate. This usually takes place between C-8 weeks and C-4 weeks, which allows enough time for customer input to influence the formation of the agenda, presentations, and discussion topics.

With personal interviews, the interviewer (usually either the CAB manager or the CAB facilitator) explores customer priorities, solicits "hot topic" discussion ideas, and asks customers to respond to proposed agenda themes. The online survey, on the other hand, is a tool used for fine-tuning an already formed agenda and gathering some specific information in advance of the meeting.

In either case, a formal agenda including customer input can now be crafted, socialized, and ratified with your company leaders and subject matter experts. You do not need to do both, but some form of pre-CAB customer interaction can be very beneficial to forming and confirming an engaging agenda that addresses both topics of high customer interest and critical relevance to your company. Here are some guidelines:

Personal interviews:
- Set expectations for needing only 20 minutes for a short interview. You'll be surprised that many will actually engage you longer. (But if you ask for 30 or 45 minutes, some customers won't offer you their time.)
- Follow an interview guide, not a script. This means that the input gathered from every customer may be

a bit different. This is okay and even expected, since no two customers are exactly alike.

- A typical interview guide consists of six or seven open-ended questions.
- Be flexible. Even with an interview guide, the customer may offer you something you haven't thought of. You may want to abandon the interview guide in order to pursue that line of questioning.
- You don't actually need to interview all the CAB attendees; a representative group of key opinion leaders will be enough to help you confirm the agenda.

Online survey:
- Ten to 12 multiple choice questions are typical, making analysis easy.
- An online survey should take only five to 10 minutes for the customer to answer.
- All questions must be relevant to the proposed agenda topics and must be stated in clear, descriptive terms; avoid ambiguous or vague questions.
- These questions allow the subject-matter experts to gather quantitative data that can be incorporated into their topic presentations.

5. Content development

When it comes to preparing CAB discussion topics it is tempting to cull slides from existing presentations, but that is exactly what customers want to avoid. They want *discussions that invite their participation, not presentations that tell*. So before firing up Microsoft PowerPoint™, take a few minutes to consider the following:

Agenda creation:

Agenda topics were first brainstormed during the kickoff meeting. However, the detailed work on the agenda doesn't begin until around C-10 weeks. By then the CAB objectives will have been defined and agreed upon by the CAB sponsor and the executive staff. In addition, the customer invitation list will have been created and the invitation process well under way. The objectives define the invitation list, and the invitation list guides the final selection of questions your leadership team will want to ask these customers. Even so, expect the agenda to evolve over the next five or six weeks. This is not a bad thing. Outside forces, industry trends, and customer input are important ingredients to building a compelling final agenda. You'll want the agenda locked by C-6 weeks.

Discussion abstracts:

The last thing customers want is to be lectured. They attend CABs because they want to be part of a strategic conversation with your executive leaders. Once the agenda is structured and an owner is assigned to each discussion topic, the next step is to think about the most valuable conversation you want to have on each topic with these customers. *What is it that your team wants to learn most from each discussion?* To avoid the knee-jerk reaction of throwing slides together, ask each discussion owner to produce a "discussion abstract" (see chapter 6). Discussion abstracts are first drafted at C-9 weeks and should be agreed upon by C-6 weeks. There is no point developing a presentation until you know the objective of that presentation and agree that it meets everyone's expectations.

Presentations:

With few exceptions, the presentations your team will make during the CAB meeting should be short with no more than a handful of slides. *Work on presentations should not begin until after the agenda and the discussion abstracts are outlined and agreed upon.* Topic owners who follow this approach find that it takes them much less time to produce the final materials. Drafting the actual slides usually begins around C-6 weeks and ideally concludes by C-3 weeks. This timeframe allows the topic owners to make use of customer input and feedback collected from either the customer interviews or pre-CAB survey which should be completed by C-5 weeks.

Each topic owner creates his or her presentation individually. However, the job of the CAB manager is to ensure that all the pieces fit well together in a logical order. CAB managers own the final master deck, which should be locked no later than C-2 weeks.

Facilitator's guide:

A facilitator's guide is a helpful tool used to gently direct each discussion topic. This tool is created for use by the facilitator. It is not something that is shared with the customers. Produced as either a short reference document or series of note cards that include the key questions relevant to each topic, the facilitator uses it to keep the discussion focused. It ensures that the facilitator is in sync with the topic owners, creating a bond of partnership between the two. If you hire a professional facilitator, he or she will produce the facilitator's guide. If you use an internal resource to facilitate the meeting, the CAB manager can create the guide.

<u>Evaluation form:</u>

The CAB represents a single vignette in the ongoing dialog your company is having with its best customers. With that in mind, it is important to review the success of the meeting and determine what improvements are required for the next meeting. A simple evaluation form will suffice. (See chapter 8 for an example.)

<u>Output reports:</u>

Upon conclusion of the CAB meeting, produce two final reports: the CAB Plan-of-Record and the CAB Executive Summary. Each serves a specific purpose explored further in Chapter 8. Complete a detailed CAB Plan-of-Record shortly after the close of the meeting while the information is still fresh in everyone's mind. A much shorter, "customer friendly" CAB Executive Summary is easy to generate after creating the CAB Plan-of-Record. Distribute this to CAB attendees as early as C+2 weeks.

2: SELECTING CUSTOMERS

What came first, the CAB or the executive relationship? It is not surprising to hear of executives choosing to forego a CAB because they don't yet have a relationship with the key customer executives they want to invite. Obviously, CABs work exceptionally well when those key executive-to-executive relationships are already in place. Yet, when those relationships do not yet exist, the CAB is a perfect forum to initiate them. So, how do you decide which individuals to invite?

The right companies

The CAB is an elite group of a dozen or so strategic customers who come together to provide guidance and direction to your company. But what does the word *strategic* really mean? Many people think of a strategic customer as a company that brings you the most revenue. And that, indeed, is one definition. However there are other dimensions of customer "strategic-ness" to consider:

- **Brand name recognition:** Invite those companies that have the most clout in their marketplace, regardless of how much business they do with your company.

- **Growth:** Learn from customers who may not be the biggest revenue producers for you today, but who represent significant growth opportunities because their business or industry is growing.

- **Innovation:** Regardless of size, create a CAB of companies who are doing interesting things with your products, services and technologies.

- **Crosspollination:** If your business spans multiple segments, invite representatives from each so as to encourage them to share best practices and explore new ideas.

There is no right or wrong answer. Use your own judgment because "strategic-ness" resides in the eye of the beholder and your specific CAB objectives.

The right contact from the right company

Selecting the right company is only the first step to building your invitation list; the next step is to invite the *right contact*. Because this is an elite group of forward-thinking individuals, it is critical that every member share a similar leadership level and a common set of responsibilities. Never underestimate the power of peer networks. This is, in fact, the number one reason why executives join CABs. (And this is why you should never allow your invited customers to delegate their attendance to an underling.) The right executive contact is a decision maker with a set of responsibilities shared with the other customer leaders. Don't rely on job titles because they are inconsistent. For example, one company hosted a CAB consisting of individuals responsible for architecting the future of their IT network. Sitting around the table were executives who had titles ranging from CIO, to VP of networks, VP of operations, and general manager. Titles varied, but they shared the responsibility.

It is equally important that the right contact be comfortable and capable of engaging with the other CAB members. The chemistry needs to work. If the right company is available but the right contact is an introvert uncomfortable with contributing in a group discussion, then that isn't a good fit. Don't invite that person, and do not then invite a lower level individual. That would create two problems: you'll offend the executive who should have been invited; and you'll annoy the other CAB members because you invited a junior member to sit with this elite executive team. Their response will be to delegate their future attendance to a lower level individual, as well. This will make your CAB initiative far less effective. If the right contact is not available, don't look for an alternative from that company. Instead, move on to the next company on your list.

Building your invitation list

Here are five suggestions for building your invitation list for CAB membership:

1. **The CAB sponsor and CAB manager are responsible for developing the invitation list and managing the invitation process** (see chapter 3). Others will provide you with solicited and unsolicited nominations and feedback, but the CAB sponsor and CAB manager are the final decision makers regarding who receives an invitation.

2. **Attending the CAB is not a perk to be given away by sales reps.** However, sales reps may nominate customers that fit a CAB profile you've predefined. Nominations should be made to the CAB sponsor and CAB manager, and these should include the name of the company, the name of specific customer executive to be invited, and the reason for the nomination. Sales reps should not communicate anything to the customer about the CAB until and unless an official invitation is awarded.

3. **Develop two lists of customer attendees:** a tier 1 list of twelve first-choice customers, and a tier 2 list consisting of a second dozen customer contacts to tap if the tier 1 list is exhausted before all the available spaces are taken. Since the CAB is a small intimate group consisting of about a dozen customer attendees, it's best to cherry pick the ideal customers first before casting a wider net. This mitigates the risk of too many customers accepting the invitation.

4. **Invite only one executive from each company**. When you invite multiple executives from the same company, you create an unbalanced playing field. A customer with three attending executives has three times the presence as a single representation from another company. It's awkward and distracting. Other customers will wonder if they could have brought additional participants.

5. **Do not mix partners or prospects with your customers.** CABs are for customers. Non-customers have a completely different set of issues, expectations, and history with your company. When companies include

non-customers in the mix, the meeting dynamics change. Somebody will walk away disappointed.

3: THE INVITATION PROCESS

See if you can spot the differences between these two styles of invitations.

Email #1
Subject line: Would you be interested in joining our CAB?

Dear (customer executive):

We're thinking of hosting a Customer Advisory Board later this year and we'd like to know if you'd be interested in joining us. We're looking for your help to guide our product roadmap as we explore areas for future growth. Your opinions are important to us, and we're interested to hear how we are doing. Please let me know if you are interested in participating, and we'll provide additional details on the event and agenda in the weeks that follow.

Best regards,

Marketing Manager

Email #2
Subject line: An invitation to join our customer advisory board

Dear (customer executive):

We are excited about kicking off our Customer Advisory Board (CAB) initiative and I would like to personally invite you to join this elite group of executive decision makers representing some of today's leading-edge companies. This invitation-only group meets once or twice a year to network, explore important business topics together, and provide us with directional guidance. You'll also learn more details about our business strategies and roadmaps. We care about what you think, and the CAB provides a perfect opportunity for us to work together.

As space is limited, please let me know if you are interested and available to participate. Our first meeting is tentatively scheduled for October 7 in Orlando. A member of my staff will be contacting you shortly to provide additional details about CAB membership and answer any questions you may have.

I hope you can join us as a member of our CAB.

Sincerely,

CEO

Let's explore what is actually going on in both emails. Invitations similar to that illustrated in email #1 fail to produce many responses because of the following reasons:

- **The subject line is weak.** Although it is a legitimate question, it feels like a plea rather than an invitation. It's easy to ignore.
- **The tone of the email conveys uncertainty.** "We're thinking of hosting a CAB...." Customers are likely to trash the email and wait for a time when the host company is certain. Customers are busy people and they don't want to waste time on concepts or ideas that may not yet be real.
- **The email is all about the host company.** It's "me, me, me"; please help us with our roadmap; tell us how we are doing. Now, this is indeed the output we want, but we can't communicate it this way because it's self-serving. This email puts the product, not the customer, in the center of the universe. There is no hint of the value customers will receive for attending.
- **There is a mismatch between the strategic nature of the CAB and the sender of the invitation.** If we expect senior executives to participate in a strategic conversation, the invitation must come from a high-ranking official, not a first-line manager.

On the other hand, invitations similar in style to that shown in email #2 work much better because they convey the right tone and set expectations more appropriately.

- **The subject line is descriptive.** It spells out "customer advisory board" (which is very important if the invitee is unfamiliar with the CAB acronym).
- **The tone is definitive and engaging.** They are not *just thinking* about hosting a CAB; they are indeed hosting a CAB. The email projects a sense of confidence, excitement, and business relevance. The tone also correctly positions the CAB as an elite group of leaders concerned about exploring topics of mutual interest. The implications are clear: being invited to join such a group is notable.
- **The email is customer-centric, not product-centric.** The CAB's value to the customer is prioritized: an opportunity to network, explore important business topics together, and provide us with directional guidance.
- **This email comes from the desk of the CEO.** It's a personal invitation from one executive to another, and it's the first step in establishing a peer-to-peer relationship at the executive level.
- **It sets expectations regarding CAB membership.** The CAB is not a single meeting or a special event. It's a serious initiative that carries some terms and conditions. The fine print of membership details is not included in the invitation email; however, they may be shared in an attachment that can be distributed to customers once they express interest in learning more. These details include membership term, roles and responsibilities, expectations, and a non-disclosure agreement.

Tips for inviting customers

A successful invitation process requires more than just a simple email. Here are five tactical tips to improve response rates and membership acceptances.

1. **Eight is the magic number for a "go/no-go" decision.** A minimum of eight confirmed customers is required to ensure the CAB meeting is a good use of time for both your company and the attending customers. CABs with fewer than eight customer attendees feel light, and it is very hard to sense any patterns from a group this small. Ideally, you'll want a dozen customers, but when making the "go / no-go" decision about a CAB meeting, eight is the minimum number. Once you confirm eight attendees, don't stop. Keep the invitation process going until you reach at least a dozen. That way, if a few customers decline at the last minute, you'll still have the minimum number to ensure a productive meeting. You can have as many as 16 customers attend, but beware of customer groups larger than 16. Bigger groups are less intimate. And the agenda segments will need to be longer to allow all participants to engage equally. This means you'll have to limit the number of topics on the agenda. In short, aim for a dozen customers, and be comfortable with a final range between eight and 16.

2. **Give customers as much notice as possible.** You don't need to wait to invite customers because you don't yet know all the details about the meeting date, venue, and agenda. The objectives of the initial invitation are to a) confirm their interest in participating in the CAB, and b) determine if the target date that works for your executive team also works for them. Your invitation

email indicates that more details will follow. In fact, you'll be nurturing a dialog with these customers over the next several months. Future customer communications will repeat the date and venue of the meeting, provide information about the agenda, and offer assistance when confirming their travel plans.

3. **Ghostwrite the invitation email for your CEO.** Set up a unique email address for the CEO specifically for CAB purposes – something that you can control and monitor without it clogging your CEO's regular inbox.

4. **Nurture a dialog with these customers.** As good as the email invitation is, it is not enough to ensure success because many emails go unread. To speed your conversion rate of CAB acceptances, a good best practice is to assign an executive to each customer invitee. Ask them to make a personal phone call to their designated contact(s) within 48 hours of the invitation being distributed. They should leave a voicemail message paraphrasing the invitation if they don't connect live. This executive-to-executive outreach solidifies both the personal relationships and strategic nature of the CAB. It shows that you are treating the CAB as a serious investment and that you care deeply about what your customers think. If possible, assign executives who already have a relationship with the targeted customer. Or, you may choose to have a sales rep or account manager follow-up. If you pursue the latter, make sure that the sales rep clearly understands that the CAB is not a sales meeting, and that he or she is acting on behalf of the CEO.

5. **Know when to move from the tier 1 list to the tier 2 list.** After a week to 10 days you will have heard from most of the invited customers, either via email or in the phone follow-ups. For the few remaining stragglers, the CAB manager can make one last attempt via email to connect with the customer. If still no response, pass over that name and replace it with a representative from the second list. Then the invitation process starts anew with the new contact.

4: SELECTING THE VENUE

The venue conducive for the most effective CAB meeting represents *neutral ground*, where all customers and company executives are treated as equals. Consider three critical components when choosing a venue: the city and location for the meeting, the hotel, and the restaurant for the network reception and dinner. These three components may be part of a single package contracted with a hotel, or they may represent three different vendors and venues. Either way, here's what to look for:

Should we host the meeting at headquarters?

While this may seem like an intuitive way to cut costs, there are three reasons why this usually isn't the best choice. First, it gives you an unfair advantage. It's the equivalent of inviting guests to your home for dinner. Most guests will be polite, following the guidelines of Emily Post etiquette. They will complement your décor even if they don't prefer it; they will refrain from disagreeing with you for fear their comments may come across as disrespectful; and some will be so uncomfortable that they choose to remain silent. It's your house; you set the rules; you drive the discussion. It's no longer neutral territory.

Second, it increases the temptation for your executives to pop in and out of the meeting. They will constantly be wondering about a meeting happening upstairs or a short conversation they need to have with someone at the end of the hall. They'll whisper, "I'll just step out for a minute; let me know what I miss." It's just too easy for your executives to multitask. This behavior is disrespectful to customers and disruptive to the entire purpose of the CAB.

And third and most dangerous, familiarity can sometimes come across as arrogance or even contempt. Executives may be completely unaware of the small changes in their body language or choice of words. The fact that you are hosting the meeting in your beautiful customer briefing center adds to some executives' confidence, making their bias even more pronounced. Arrogance is the one trait that will doom any meaningful discussion. And this is very hard to control when it rears its ugly head. Because of these three reasons, it's best to hold the CAB meeting offsite.

Choose an easy-to-get-to location

The cost of the venue is always a top concern; however, there are others that require special thought. The city and location of the CAB must be easy for your customers to get to. It should be in close proximity to a major airport, ideally within a 45-minute drive. Some US CAB-friendly cities include Chicago (during the spring and fall, never winter), Dallas, Las Vegas, New Orleans, Orlando (spring and fall, but watch out for hurricane season), Salt Lake City, and San Francisco. It's easy to get direct flights in and out of these cities; ground transportation is abundant; and the weather is typically good. Favorite European cities include the usual suspects of London, Paris, Frankfurt, and Rome. Your selection of the ideal venue will also depend on where the majority of your customers are located and if there are other events taking place that they will want to attend at the same time. Some companies chose to hold their CABs in major metropolitan areas like New York City, but care must be taken that difficulties getting to and from the airport are minimized. If most of the customers reside in New York City, then that's one thing; however, do you want your out-of-town customers sitting in NYC traffic for 90 minutes trying to get from JFK airport to SoHo? It's never good when customers arrive feeling hassled and tired because of a difficult journey. Try to make it easy for them.

The CAB is not a vacation, but . . .

Your customers are coming to take part in an important business meeting, not play. Regardless, depending on the relationship you have with these customers, and depending on when flights are available for arrival or departure, you may want to invite them to participate in an extracurricular activity. There is no expectation on your customers' part to do so, but here are a few extras some companies have included:

- A call center company hosted their CAB in the city of one of their best customers. Based in Nashville, the Home Shopping Network offered a tour of their facility to all customers arriving early for the CAB meeting. The tour of HSN and how they manage their call center was very relevant to the other customers. This optional activity proved to be an excellent pre-CAB event that energized all participants.

- A hi-tech company held their CAB in Orlando at the newly opened Ritz-Carlton. Because of the economic slow down, they were able to negotiate a very favorable rate for all accommodations, including a round of golf for the subset of customers eager to play at this prestigious course.

- A premier logistics and transportation company well known in Dallas was granted special access to the Dallas Cowboy Stadium. They offered customers a behind-the-scenes tour of the facilities for all interested customers. Half of the attending customers made special arrangements to arrive early to take part in this activity.

The conference room

The meeting room must provide a comfortable, professional ambience that meets the expectations of this group. The room must be clean, well lit, and have windows that allow for natural light. The room must also be big enough so no one feels claustrophobic. One customer recalled a particularly uncomfortable meeting room: "It was long, narrow, and included no windows. I felt like we were held hostage. I couldn't wait to get out of there."

The CAB requires an environment for collaboration, not a classroom. The room must allow for a U-shaped table around which every customer and company executive and the facilitator can sit. It's very important that everyone is treated as an equal during the meeting. Avoid auditorium-style or tiered seating which forces everyone to face forward instead of each other and is not conducive to interactive discussions.

You'll also need a projector and two flip charts, one placed in each of the two front corners of the room. A table set in the back of the room should contain coffee and other drinks, but food should not be allowed in the meeting room. Breakfast or lunch aromas soon turn odorous if left standing all day. The presence of food also creates opportunities for spills and other messes best left in a separate dining area. Lastly, you want to minimize interruptions from the hotel staff and the noise that accompanies the arrival and removal of food carts, trays, and dinnerware.

Seating arrangements

The general rule is that there should be two customers to every one company executive. So, if twelve customers attend, there can be six host company executives, plus a facilitator. (Logistics coordinators aren't included in this count because their work is largely behind the scenes.) That means that you'll be looking for a meeting room that can hold 20-25 people. Never have more company executives at the table than customers because it creates an unbalanced atmosphere where customers will feel outnumbered. Take care to intermix customers with the executive staff; having customers sit on one side of the table while the executives sit facing them creates an atmosphere more akin to interrogation. Instead, follow this general layout: the facilitator sits at one of the open ends of the U-shaped table near the screen; the CAB Sponsor sits at the other open end; customers and company executives are shuffled together so no two company executives sit next to each other, if possible. And everyone should have a name plate or tent card that is readable from the other side of the table.

CABs are unique meetings, and many people in your company will want to attend. It's best to avoid this expectation. The CAB meeting establishes a sense of equality where everyone sits at the table. When companies allow staff members to stand at the back of the room, it creates a viewing gallery that could easily become an unwelcome distraction. Keep the group small and intimate. Remind staff members that notes will be taken and information will be shared after the meeting (see chapter 8).

Dining and breakout rooms

Use a separate room nearby for breakfast and lunch. These private rooms allow for the dialog to continue during breaks. Don't use public restaurants for the CAB meeting because it will be impossible for customers to speak freely, and the noise level will be too loud. If the agenda requires the team split into smaller breakout teams, you'll need at least one additional room. The additional room may be the same one you use for breakfast and lunch. The only requirement is that it also be private and available for use all day.

Hotel rooms

Your customers expect a clean comfortable room. Suites are not required. Again, choose a hotel that is consistent with the needs and expectations of your customers. If your customers tend to prefer traditional settings, choose a hotel, such as the St. Francis Hotel in San Francisco or the Ritz-Carlton in Orlando. These hotels are more formal and professionally well-suited for business travelers and meetings. If your attendees are more avant-garde, you might select a hotel that is more boutique-ish (although be sure they have appropriate meeting space).

Network reception, dinner, and after hours entertainment

Sometimes you can find a hotel with a very nice restaurant. Other times you may want to host the reception in a separate location. Either works as long as the reception and dinner are held in a private room.

The benefit of hosting the network reception and dinner at the hotel is that no further travel is required and latecomers don't need to be transported separately. Holding the meeting at a location that also offers nightlife encourages conversations to continue over drinks or a show. In fact, the most insightful conversations often happen not at the meeting but during lunch, dinner or after-hours. You'll want to allow for this type of interaction to take place freely.

If you decide to hold your reception or dinner at a different location other than the hotel property, you'll need to provide ground transportation. Customers don't want to sit in a van for an hour just to get to a restaurant, so choose a location that is nearby. A 15-minute ride is acceptable; avoid anything longer. And plan ahead to deal with any late arrivals.

Menu

Dietary needs vary greatly. Make sure vegetarian and vegan options are available. Inquire with your customers early to find out if they have any food preferences, requirements or restrictions; that way, you and they will avoid embarrassment at dinner. At a CAB meeting in Germany the dinner was held in a beautiful castle where all attendees were surrounded by history and art. The host company wanted to treat the customers to an assortment of extravagant, rich dishes consistent with the castle's history. Unfortunately, the menu was not familiar (or digestible) to many of the foreign attendees. The ambiance was fantastic, but many dishes remained untouched, and jokes about the unidentifiable food were whispered during breaks the next day.

Dress code

Dress code is business casual for all attendees. As a matter of standard etiquette, slacks and a sports coat are standard for men, ties are not required, and jeans are not appropriate. Women may wear a blouse with either slacks or a skirt; again jeans are not appropriate.

5: BUILDING THE AGENDA

The CAB's objectives drive the agenda, not the other way around. Once you and your team have a shared understanding of what you want to achieve, then you can start focusing on the details.

An agenda for your first CAB meeting

The inaugural CAB meeting is especially important because it marks the first opportunity not only to introduce the CAB initiative, but also to establish a baseline understanding of the vision and mission that drives your company. For running a *first* meeting, the following agenda is the most effective. Agenda suggestions for successive, more advanced CAB meetings are included at the end of this chapter.

Day 1: Focus on introductions
- Afternoon arrival
- *If offered:* pre-CAB social event (golf, tour of customer facility, etc.). Any pre-CAB social event is optional for customers
- Reception
- Informal dinner

The intention here is to introduce the players so you don't have to spend time on this during the main meeting, saving as much as 45 minutes on the next day's agenda. More importantly, the customers will arrive on Day 2 having some familiarity with each other, thus feeling more relaxed when it comes to interacting and sharing their perspectives during the day.

It is not required that your company sponsor a pre- or post-CAB social event, such as golf or other outing. If you do choose to offer a social event, it is customary to make it optional to the attending customers. Some will gladly accept the invitation if their travel schedules permit; however, their time is valuable, so it's best not to make them feel obliged to attend.

Day 2: The main event
- 7:30 – Breakfast
- 8:30 – Welcome and CAB overview
- 8:45 – "Trends & drivers" discussion
- 9:25 – Host company's strategy & vision presentation
- 10:00 – Break
- 10:30 – Discussion topic #1
- 11:15 – Discussion topic #2
- 12:00 – Lunch (no agenda)
- 1:00 – Discussion topic #3
- 1:45 – Discussion topic #4
- 2:30 – Break
- 2:45 – Customer prioritization exercise
- 3:15 – Closing comments
- 3:30 – Adjourn

Day 2 ends at 3:30 pm. Shouldn't we go all day? The simple answer is no. The higher the seniority of the attending customers, the less time they have in their schedules for you. There is nothing worse than having one or two customers leave in the middle of a discussion to catch a plane. It's disruptive and awkward for the remaining customers who will then start looking at their watches. For the first CAB meeting, keep the agenda short. This allows ample time for customers to catch a flight home that evening. The best feedback received in many CAB evaluations was, "I wish we had more time!" Always leave them wanting more. This is a testament to an engaging, valuable agenda. This remark also serves as an open invitation for marketing and sales folks to follow-up with CAB members to continue the dialog long after the meeting has adjourned.

Why this agenda works

It's all about the customers. They attend CAB meetings because they are eager to network with their peers and to discuss and compare notes regarding key trends, drivers, and issues that shape their businesses. Customer executives have few opportunities to do this, and vendors who take the time to build an agenda around customer-facing issues will be rewarded with high attendance. Customers want to talk, so let them. Let's break down the pieces of this agenda:

The **Welcome & CAB overview** is the required preamble to remind customers why they are here, what topics will be covered, and the appropriate rules of engagement. The CEO or CAB sponsor will open the meeting, expressing delight and thanks to the attending customers. They will then introduce the facilitator who will review the agenda and introduce the first discussion topic.

The first discussion module, typically described as a **"trends & drivers" discussion,** explores a customer-focused, industry-level business perspective. What trends, drivers, and priorities are shaping their businesses? What "big picture" influences do these customers care about?

This is a conversation, not a presentation. However, we do want to ensure the discussion is relevant, so it must be carefully set up. You've read the analyst reports and have your own opinion of the industry. But, is your assessment synergistic with that of your customers? If not, your business may be in trouble. To begin the conversation, summarize three trends and drivers you believe are most relevant. Pull slides from a recent analyst report or summarize an article you read in the *Wall Street Journal* or other relevant publication. Construct three slides, each one revealing a specific, well-illustrated point. The more interesting, thought provoking or controversial, the better. Then, step back and allow the customers to respond. Your job is not to defend these trends, but to watch and assess how your customers respond to the hypotheses you've just described. Pay close attention to the themes that emerge so you can weave them into the conversations that follow.

We've just heard from customers on how they see the world; now it's your turn, and your response is presented in the form of a **company overview.** Since this is the first CAB meeting, it is safe to assume that the attending customers may not share a common understanding of the value your company offers. The objective of this presentation is to establish a common frame of reference, and it's appropriate for your CEO to be the speaker. While this is a company overview, this is not your "corporate pitch" or set of slides you routinely present at other events or sales meetings. CAB customers want and expect more; they want to be invited into your inner circle to know what's really going on. As such, the CEO needs to present his or her company in a less-formal, more-casual "fireside chat"-type manner. Plan on a 20-minute presentation using as few slides as possible. Having listened carefully to the "trends & drivers" discussion, the quick-footed CEO will be able to establish relevance by relating the company's value proposition using words and phrasing consistent with the customers' interests.

You may wonder if these two "presentations" should be reversed. The answer is no. Frankly, it's safer to have the customers share their business view first for two reasons. The first is that customers have come to the CAB because they believe you want to hear their opinions, not sit quietly while you pitch to them. So, let them speak first. But the second reason is much more prudent: Imagine if the customers' view of industry trends and drivers was different from your own. If the CEO spoke first, he or she would not know that. That could create some awkward moments later. When the customers speak first, if they share some surprising perspectives or priorities, the CEO now has a chance to respond to them and mold his or her comments accordingly. The CEO can't do that if he or she speaks first.

Break #1 is thirty minutes long. As valuable as you believe your agenda will be, often times the most important eye-opening conversations happen during the breaks and lunch. A long morning break is important for delivering a relaxing, but packed, CAB experience that nurtures relationships. And, yes, this break also gives your team time to check their email.

Up until now, the day's agenda has been carefully scripted. Customize **topics #1 - #4** for your business. Said another way, you have a three-hour block of time in which to address whatever topics you want. But there are some rules to remember: Don't focus on problem solving, and don't delve into the finer details of specific features. Instead, appropriate topics explore potential new investment areas, services, or product offerings. Rather than focusing on specific tactical features, ask customers how they view and prioritize various problem statements that your company might choose to address. No topic is off limits as long as it is consistent with the goals and objectives for the CAB.

While you don't want to rush through a series of questions, it is important to manage your time wisely. Use the CAB to explore, verify, or brainstorm answers to questions you care about. Be focused, and end each discussion either with a conclusion or identification of next steps that will allow the conversation to continue after the meeting adjourns.

There is no agenda during **lunch**. As with the morning and afternoon breaks, lunch needs to be an informal time where customers can sit together to continue side conversations with each other and members of your staff. Conduct topic #3 and #4 discussions after lunch.

Imagine a meeting room surrounded by annotated flipchart sheets taped to the walls. A lot of information and ideas have been captured. If we leave the meeting now, your team may have trouble separating out the most important suggestions and considerations. That's why the final topic of the day is a **prioritization and ranking exercise**.

This exercise can unfold in one of two ways: In one common variation, preparing for this exercise begins during the afternoon break. At that time, the facilitator and CAB sponsor surveys the flipcharts in order to create a short-list of the most relevant ideas. When the customers return, you ask them to vote on the suggestions they believe your company should prioritize. Or, give them $100 of play money and ask them to spread their investment among the ideas. In tallying up the totals, the most important ideas will become obvious.

A second variation puts complete control in the customers' hands. Here, the facilitator invites all company executives to leave the room. He or she splits the customer group into two smaller teams and asks each to draft of list five recommendations for the host company's consideration. Each small team shares their thoughts with the other, and a final list of five recommendations is then prioritized. When the company executives rejoin the group, the list is revealed. The customer who drafted each of the prioritized items reads it to the group and provides additional commentary. The executives may ask clarifying questions at this time. Problem solving is not allowed. Company executives thank the customers for this valuable input and can explore the implications later back at the office and in follow-up conversations with selected CAB members.

At 3:30 pm, the meeting adjourns. Whatever agenda you set, it is most imperative that the meeting starts and ends on time. Honor these customers by acknowledging their time and thanking them for their contributions. In the closing remarks, made by the facilitator, CAB sponsor, and CEO (in that order), reaffirm the value of the discussions and how this customer input will be used to help guide your company.

Agenda variations for subsequent CAB meetings

With a successful inaugural CAB meeting under your belt, you now have a lot of credibility with your CAB members. They understand how these meetings work and will be eager to continue the dialog, giving you a lot more flexibility regarding the breadth and depth of your next agenda. Based on the synchronized interest of your customers and your executive staff, you may decide to augment your next CAB meeting with some of the following:

- A longer agenda, either running a full-day or a day-and-a-half.
- Breakouts where subgroups can explore a topic in more detail.
- An actual "work session" where customers can team up with you to work on an issue or build a plan.
- Customer-led discussions about use cases or best practices.
- A guest speaker, such as an industry analyst or noted author, who brings a unique perspective and relevant information that adds to the CAB objectives. Industry updates or new ideas presented by guest speakers can be a thought-provoking setup leading into a brainstorming or other breakout session.

There is no end to the creativity you can introduce into your CAB agendas. The only condition is that the agenda remains consistent with and relevant to your central objective. Doing so will provide you and your team with meaningful input to make the best business decisions possible.

6: PREPARING CAB PRESENTATIONS

The most successful CAB presentations are not assembled from existing materials. They are carefully sculpted based on the questions the team is most eager to ask. Before the team sets out to construct any slide presentation, invite them to consider three key planning questions:

1. What is the objective of your topic?
2. What is the outline of your presentation and how do you envision the discussion and interaction that will follow?
3. What specific questions do you want to ask, or what assumptions do you want to validate?

Completing this simple template takes about 20 minutes. Its purpose is to help the topic owner achieve the desired outcome from his or her conversation with CAB members. Some people may view this step as extra work. However, it actually saves time because it forces topic owners to focus, making it much easier to create and edit the presentation. Figure 2 offers an example drafted by an executive preparing for his discussion topic.

Customer Advisory Board
Discussion Abstract

Working Title: The Evolving Priorities in Supply Chain Management

Discussion leader(s): John Doe ☐ Tentative ☑ Firm

1. Objectives: *What are your goals for this discussion module? What outcomes are you seeking from the interactive discussion? (e.g., validate business direction, brainstorm future investment areas, explore customer priorities)*

Example: The objective of this discussion is to validate assumptions regarding how customers are tracking products globally across their entire supply chain. This is a "use case" discussion. We want to explore a "day in the life" of the logistics manager so we better understand their top 3 pain points. We also want to learn from customers how they are actually using our products and services.

2. Summary: *Provide an executive summary of the material to be covered. What is the focus of the presentation and facilitated CAB discussion? What topics and content will be covered?*

Example: Businesses are tightening their expectations for just-in-time delivery of products, with more manufacturing and packaging steps being moved from the manufacturing floor to warehousing/distribution centers. This discussion module is focused on understanding how and why these expectations are likely to change over the next 3 years, and how these changes will impact (positively and negatively) their ability to track products globally across the entire supply chain. We'll begin the discussion by summarizing what we believe to be the top 3 issues and then ask the customers to elaborate. Then we'll unveil our product roadmap and ask them to verify which functionality is most important to them and why.

3. Questions to be asked or assumptions to be validated: *List 5 questions and/or assumptions you want to test. What, exactly, do you want to learn from this session?*

Example questions:
1) What are the top 3 supply chain priorities TODAY regarding operations, tracking & reporting?

2) How are these priorities likely to change OVER THE NEXT 3 YEARS?

3) What decision criteria do customers use when selecting a transportation/ logistics partner?

4) We are evaluating options to enhance our reporting services to include A and B. What values do you associate with either of these potential options?

5) If we could do one thing to dramatically improve your supply chain operations, what would you ask us to do?

Figure 2: An example of a discussion abstract.

When drafting slides, here are a few tips to keep in mind:

- Limit the number of slides to the fewest needed to set up the conversation. Customers don't evaluate the value of any presentation based on the number of slides. They value the interaction that follows.

- Make sure your slides are readable from the back of the room. The minimum font size should be 18 pt. As a test, print out your slides (one per page) and place them on the floor. From a standing position, can you read the slide? If you can't, it means your typeface is too small.

- Graphics speak louder than words. Don't use run-on sentences crammed into a block of text. Include an image with some short bullet points. Speak to the points you want to make. Try not to read from the slide when presenting.

- If your topic requires more detailed information, distribute handouts for customers to review before the meeting. These can be distributed with the CAB welcome package (see page 80) they receive upon checking in at the hotel. Or, you can provide a short pre-reading assignment for the attending customers. If given enough warning, customers will come prepared by reading any materials you give them in advance.

- Include an audience-engagement tactic. Customers want to be involved. Allow them to actively participate by asking them questions at key points during your presentation, not just at the end. Other forms of interaction include letting them vote on alternatives, brainstorm ideas on sticky notes then tape them on the walls, and participating in an impromptu panel discussion. There's also no reason why your team needs to do all of the presenting. Ask customers to co-present the material with you. There are many options.

- If you aren't sure how to liven up your discussion module, don't hesitate to work with your facilitator. A good facilitator will help you match the most effective customer-engagement technique to achieve your objective. They can also help you complete the discussion abstract template and brainstorm creative ways to drive the dialog so you achieve the valuable outcome you seek.

7: MAKING THE CASE FOR A PROFESSIONAL FACILITATOR

Running a successful CAB meeting yourself isn't as easy as it sounds, especially when you need to balance managing the meeting while actively participating in it. Partnering with a professional facilitator can help you do both. Whether you decide to facilitate your own CAB meeting, or hire an outside expert, this chapter provides some helpful context.

Meeting facilitation takes place when an unbiased person assists an organization in conducting productive and engaging discussions involving multiple parties, participants, and complex issues. An effective facilitator's work begins long before the start of the meeting. He or she guides the host company's leadership team in preparing an engaging agenda of relevant topics and questions. During the CAB meeting, the facilitator sets a positive tone and a comfortable atmosphere that encourages customers to participate fully.

Professional facilitators, precisely because they don't wear a company badge, can ask the difficult questions your executives may want to ask but may be uncomfortable asking. Gently and diplomatically, the facilitator guides the group so there is a balanced level of interaction from all customers and your company's executives don't dominate the meeting. He or she remains neutral, always focused on the customers. The professional facilitator seeks to understand the core issues, without regards to company politics.

However, when an internal leader assumes the role of facilitator, trouble can follow despite the best of intentions. It is virtually impossible for him or her to be neutral on every issue. And it's all too common for executives to fall into a defensive posture. When executives facilitate their own CABs, they often cross the line into control and advocacy for their point of view. Customers can immediately sense this even when leaders believe they are being neutral. In response, the customers' body language and level of engagement changes. These changes (i.e. fidgeting, looking at their watches, texting or checking their email, avoiding direct eye contact) may go unnoticed by a novice facilitator. Or, worse, the leader upon sensing the change in atmosphere may attempt to compensate by speaking louder, faster, or repeating information to fill the available time. Unfortunately, that type of response is less than helpful because it pushes customers further away.

Drifting from the agenda, lack of balanced participation, and running overtime are additional shortcomings that can plague CABs when they are poorly facilitated.

Sometimes the roles of facilitator and CAB host are assumed to be one in the same. They are not. Separating the roles of CAB host and facilitator frees the executive team to spend more time listening while ensuring that one person (the facilitator) is properly focused on group dynamics, process issues, managing the agenda, and keeping customers engaged. A professional facilitator helps CAB members get to know each other, learn to cooperate, and work issues together. Simply put, a professional CAB facilitator is an unbiased discussion leader who guides the meeting forward and keeps it focused.

Whether you decide to hire a professional facilitator, or appoint an internal executive to the role, here is a short list of what you should expect from them.

The best CAB facilitators . . .
√ Work with company leaders to develop, prioritize, or refine your CAB objectives, ensuring proper linkages to the business strategy and operations plans. (Refer to *The Flipchart Guide™ to Customer Advisory Boards, Volume 1.*)

√ Recommend agenda options and the most effective customer-engagement methods and techniques for achieving the CAB objectives.

√ Coach topic owners to prepare effective presentations and discussion modules.

√ Guide the entire CAB experience, ensuring that your company's leaders and customers understand the objective of each discussion module and that a productive, valuable outcome results from the interaction.

√ Ensure that every customer feels included and has an opportunity to participate in the discussions.

√ Establish a collaborative relationship with participants by creating and sustaining an environment of trust and openness where everyone feels safe to speak honestly and where differences of opinion are respected.

√ Provide a structure for learning that includes setting rules of engagement, teeing up discussion topics, and keeping to an agenda.

√ Document the conversation flow on flipcharts (or some other visual aid) so that all participants can see, comment on, and benefit from the key points, creative thoughts, and "aha!" moments captured from the conversation in real time.

√ Co-lead or facilitate the post-mortem meetings with the CAB manager, offering feedback and recommendations to achieve further success.

But, a facilitator is not . . .

x The host or the person in charge: The CEO and CAB sponsor are the meeting's hosts; the facilitator maintains neutrality.

x A lecturer: The facilitator is a co-learner, exploring all subjects with CAB members as an equal partner.

x A content expert: A seasoned facilitator is an expert in planning and guiding the agenda to produce relevant insight and perspectives. He or she should be familiar enough with the topic areas to be conversant. A good facilitator will spend two to three months working with and learning from the host company so as to guide the most effective discussions. However, it is not necessary for the facilitator to have deep content expertise because other participants will provide that knowledge if and when it is required. The most effective facilitators provide value in asking key questions in a non-judgmental way, not defending the answers.

x   The center of attention: A good facilitator draws people into the discussion and speaks less than other participants.

x   An arbiter: In collaborative learning, no one, least of all the facilitator, determines that some opinions are "correct" or "more valid." The facilitator never advocates particular opinions, takes sides, or tries to persuade others.

When hiring a professional facilitator

CABs have become more mainstream in recent years, and there are a number of firms and consultants offering various facilitation services. But not all professional facilitators are a like. When interviewing facilitator candidates, here are seven questions to consider:

1. Is the professional facilitator focused on CAB preparation as well as actual facilitation services for business-to-business companies in your industry?

2. Does the facilitator have a proven track record of CAB facilitation success? Or, is this the first time they'll be providing this type of service?

3. What's their background? What executive leadership experience does the facilitator bring?

4. What proof points (e.g. customer success stories, best-practice articles, customer testimonials) can the facilitator share?

5. How and when will the facilitator interact with your team? What methodology does he or she follow? Is it documented?

6. Are you comfortable with the facilitator interacting one-on-one with your CEO and executive staff? Does his or her personal style and chemistry fit with your organization?

7. Do you trust him or her to deliver a balanced, interactive CAB?

8: INFORMATION CAPTURE AND DISSEMINATION

Talk is cheap. Any true value comes from actions taken after the meeting. For that to happen, the insights, feedback, and recommendations need to be captured during the meeting, then organized into a format that is easy for dissemination to CAB attendees (customers and executives) and to employees who were not present.

On the use of flipcharts

Because the CAB is structured as an interactive meeting, it's important to capture feedback in a way that is visible to everyone. While this may seem old-school in an era of modern technology, the flipchart visual brings everyone together. It offers a shared experience where all participants can see, comment on, and benefit from the key points, creative thoughts and insights captured from the conversation in real time. There are several variations in the execution, but here's how it typically works.

1. The topic leader presents his or her material. Because we want customers to do 80% of the talking, it is best to ask presenters to use a minimum of slides (perhaps no more than seven). That way, we have

more time to discuss the customers' answers to the speaker's questions. During this time, the facilitator sits quietly on the sidelines.

2. Place flipcharts in the two front corners of the room (on either side of the screen). When the speaker comes to a "question slide" (or concludes the presentation), the facilitator comes forward to facilitate the response.

3. The facilitator, well aware of the objectives for each discussion module, gently guides the customer conversation without any bias. While the focus shifts from the speaker to the facilitator and customers, the speaker stays in the front of the room to provide additional information or answer clarifying questions if they arise.

4. As customers offer answers, the facilitator, using active listening techniques, notes key words and short phrases on the flipcharts.

5. The facilitator is mindful of maintaining a balanced discussion and ensures all customers have an opportunity to provide his or her thoughts. As such, he or she may direct follow-up questions to other customers who have not yet voiced a response.

6. At the conversation's conclusion, the speaker takes center stage again, scans the flipchart notes, and offers a summary of the most interesting points.

On more detailed note-taking

In addition to the facilitator jotting key words on flipcharts, it is helpful to have a designated note-taker capturing more detailed notes on a tablet or laptop computer. Taking notes is not about creating a word-for-word record of the meeting; you don't need a stenographer. The note-taker should be a content expert who understands the implications of customer comments and can annotate further when conducting a final analysis of the conversation.

When the meeting concludes, the designated note-taker and facilitator integrate their notes into a final "Plan of Record" intended for internal audiences only. A customer-friendly version of this report, following the Chatham House Rules (see page 68), is also distributed to customers. These are the only forms of note taking that are allowed. Do not videotape or record the CAB session. Video cameras and recording devices impede the conversation and make customers feel uncomfortable.

Two final reports

The most commonly forgotten or delayed step in the CAB process is the writing of the final reports. Once the meeting concludes, it is very easy for all involved to be drawn back into their jobs. Urgent matters of the day take priority, and soon days, then weeks, pass. The notes from the CAB sit quietly gathering dust in a corner until someone realizes that no report was ever written or distributed. This usually comes to light when preparations begin for the next CAB meeting. Of course, by then it is too late.

If you decide to hire a professional facilitator, he or she typically takes ownership for drafting the final set of reports: a detailed CAB Plan-of-Record for internal audiences, and a shorter CAB Executive Summary for customers. The facilitator, having worked intensely with your company for the past three or four months during the CAB planning process, is capable of summarizing the notes for you in a logical order and with enough detail to make the report useful and relevant. Then, of course, you have the opportunity to edit or embellish the report prior to distributing it to your executive team and other audiences. Since it is always easier to edit than to create, outsourcing the drafting of these final summaries to the professional facilitator is a useful way to document this information quickly while you focus on other duties.

If you decide to facilitate the meeting yourself, be sure to schedule time afterwards where you, the CAB sponsor, and the designated note taker can sit together to compare your notes and create both reports.

As a guide, here's a typical table of contents for each.

CAB Plan-of-Record (for internal use only)

This document is a detailed summary of all aspects of the CAB meeting, including who said what. Because this is an internal-use only document, the Chatham House Rule does not apply. However, it does apply to the CAB Executive Summary.

When a meeting is held under the **Chatham House Rule***, participants are free to use the information received, but neither the identity nor the affiliation of the speaker(s), nor that of any other participant, may be revealed publicly.*

The Chatham House Rule
www.chathamhouse.org

For internal purposes, it may be very helpful to know who said what. The objective of the CAB Plan-of-Record is two-fold: to be an accurate summary of the meeting including documenting the customer priorities and related recommendations they've offered your leadership team, and to be a reference tool for all employees, including those who did not attend the meeting. Employees should be able to read the document and feel that they were in the room at the time of the discussions. It is not uncommon for the detailed report to be 20 pages long. The CAB Plan-of-Record keeps the voice of the CAB alive. Typically included in this report are the following:

- Executive summary of the CAB meeting
- Date, venue of the meeting
- Meeting agenda
- List of attending customers
- Detailed summaries of each discussion topic,
- Conclusion, including a prioritized set of specific recommendations for your company's consideration
- Action-items regarding follow-up from this meeting with focus on how to keep the CAB conversation going throughout the year
- CAB evaluation results (see next section).

CAB Executive Summary (for sharing with customers)

The **CAB Executive Summary**, on the other hand, is a document prepared specifically for customers. Customers want to know they've been heard, and this document is a way to close the loop. The following contents are often included:

- Date, venue of this meeting
- Meeting agenda
- List of attending customers *(only if customers have given their expressed permission to share their contact information with each other)*
- High-level synopsis of the meeting
- Conclusion, including a prioritized set of specific recommendations offered for your company's consideration
- Date, venue, and location for the next meeting if known

The CAB Executive Summary is different from the CAB Plan-of-Record in several ways. First, it's much shorter, perhaps two to three pages long. Second, the attendee list is not included unless the customers have given their permission to share their contact information with the other CAB members. And customers are not directly identified with any specific piece of feedback they have provided. Again, this is known as the Chatham House Rule. This is done to protect the privacy of all participants and to avoid unintentionally causing embarrassment, setting expectations, or implying judgment of any kind directly associated with any comment.

Sharing the CAB Executive Summary with the attending members eliminates disappointment, and it also provides you with a reason to follow-up with them after the meeting.

Customer evaluation & post-mortem

Each CAB meeting represents a single vignette in the ongoing dialog you have with your best customers. With that in mind, it is important to review the success of the meeting and determine what improvements are required. A simple evaluation form will suffice. The evaluation may be distributed via hardcopy, email, or online.

A common practice is to print it out and distribute it to customers as part of their welcome kit. Remind customers to complete the form prior to departing. This is the only way to assure 100% participation. Figure 3 offers a generic example of what is included in an evaluation form. For companies that already have an idea of what their next year's calendar looks like, they can ask customers to "save the date" for the next meeting at the close of the current CAB meeting. Or, they may invite customers to suggest dates and venue preferences. This helps promote a sense of continuity of CAB membership from meeting to meeting.

Customer Advisory Board meeting: date

Thank you for joining us for this meeting!

Please help us make our CAB meetings as effective as possible by offering us your feedback.

Name:

Company:

Compared to other CAB meetings you've attended, how does this one rate?

❏ Better   ❏ Same   ❏ Worse   ❏ This was my first CAB

Overall, how was the meeting?	**Poor**			**Excellent**	
The topics were relevant.	1	2	3	4	5
The presentations were clear and informative.	1	2	3	4	5
It was easy to participate in the discussions.	1	2	3	4	5
I felt my input was heard and respected.	1	2	3	4	5
I enjoyed hearing from other customers.	1	2	3	4	5
I felt I had access to the executives.	1	2	3	4	5
The meeting met my expectations.	1	2	3	4	5
This was a good use of my time.	1	2	3	4	5

How valuable was each session?	**Poor**			**Excellent**	
Reception evening	1	2	3	4	5
Trends & drivers discussion	1	2	3	4	5
Company strategy overview	1	2	3	4	5
Topic #1	1	2	3	4	5
Topic #2	1	2	3	4	5
Topic #3	1	2	3	4	5
Topic #4	1	2	3	4	5

Please comment on the logistics.	**Poor**			**Excellent**	
Pre-CAB meeting communications	1	2	3	4	5
Meeting location and hotel venue	1	2	3	4	5
Meeting room (comfortable)	1	2	3	4	5
Ground transportation to/from hotel/airport	1	2	3	4	5
Food	1	2	3	4	5

What topics would you like to see discussed at a future CAB meeting?

What else could we do to ensure these meetings are valuable to you?

Any other comments?

Figure 3: An evaluation form example

The post-mortem

Conducting a quick analysis of customer evaluations during the post-mortem meeting, along with collecting immediate feedback from your executives, is very important. Because people's schedules fill up quickly, the CAB manager should plan ahead, booking time for an executive debriefing when booking the CAB meeting on the executives' calendars. As an example, one CAB manager scheduled her post-mortem meeting to take place at the meeting venue one hour after all customers had departed. She was then able to collect immediate feedback from the executives before they left the hotel. Participants in the post-mortem review include all company executives, managers, and support staff who attended the CAB meeting. Here are a few common questions discussed:

1) Did we meet the objectives we defined for this CAB meeting?

2) How effective was the agenda?

3) How did the CAB customers evaluate the meeting?

4) How did customers respond to the location (city) and venue (hotel)? Where should we hold the next meeting?

5) Was this meeting a good use of our time? Did we get the right kind of feedback?

6) What should we do differently at our next CAB meeting based on customer feedback and what we learned and experienced?

Taking action

Recognizing that CABs represent just one of the many mechanisms used to collect customer and market data, it is quite possible that the CAB will suggest actions that you will disagree with or not be prepared to implement. There is no requirement that states a host company must embrace all or even any customer requests and prescriptions. However, be sure to communicate back to the CAB participants what actions you have taken as a result of the CAB – even if the action was not pursuing a specific CAB-generated suggestion.

Your customers are smart business people and they know there are many variables that must be considered in managing your business. They actually have no expectations that you will act on their suggestions without further consideration. And so, recognizing this expectation, you owe your CAB customers an honest answer and an update on steps taken between CAB meetings. When executives ignore sharing decisions that are contrary to the CAB, or telling these customers that no action was taken since the last CAB meeting, customers quickly become disenchanted with the process. They will feel that they are wasting their time, not because you didn't do what they suggested, but because you weren't honest in communicating back to them.

The action items suggested or implied during the meeting will be broad-brush in nature. The assignment of specific, measurable actions will unfold during the post-mortem and other post-CAB meetings where the executives and product leaders explore the implications of the CAB's recommendations. This is the time when strategic planners and product leaders must clearly articulate what action items and related deadlines they will accept.

With the action items agreed upon, the CAB sponsor should then provide all employees with an update on the CAB and the next steps. This may take the form of an internal executive summary, a short article in an internal newsletter, or even a podcast to employees. This executive summary to the organization should take place within two to three weeks of the CAB meeting, while it is still fresh in memory. This is also the time to send your executive summary of the meeting to the customers who participated. Organizations have short attention spans; to wait longer makes it easier for the CAB sponsor to forget this duty.

To help maintain momentum, the CAB sponsor should assign an owner capable of working cross-functionally to track specific action items and maintain internal visibility. Some companies funnel the CAB feedback directly into the annual planning process just for this reason. This makes it easy to keep the spirit of the CAB alive and the issues fresh as you prepare for the next CAB meeting. By the way, the first discussion module in the next CAB meeting will be a review of the action items and recommendations that were generated from the prior CAB meeting. An update is required and expected.

9: SETTING A BUDGET

Let's get to the bottom line: How much does it cost to run a CAB face-to-face meeting? The answer is, of course, it depends. On average, companies will spend between $50,000 and $75,000 per CAB meeting. Typical costs include hotel, ground transportation, and meals for all participants. This is sometimes referred to as "wheels to wheels" costs, meaning that the host company covers all travel, lodging, and food costs incurred beginning when customers arrive in the city of the meeting (touchdown) and ending when customers leave on their flight home (takeoff).

What about airfare? For US-based customers, it is customary for all domestic attendees to pay their own airfare. If a host company includes one or two international customers to join a meeting of mostly-domestic CAB customers, the host company may offer to pay for international travel. However, even international customers may be unable to accept your generosity due to their company rules. Extend the offer anyway; it will be appreciated.

The primary cost components to consider in your CAB budget include the following:

- The number of attendees
- The length and number of CAB meetings per year
- Hiring a professional facilitator (or not)
- Including a guest speaker (or not)
- Network reception and formal dinner
- Food during the meeting
- Production of a CAB welcome package
- Customer appreciation gift
- Ground transportation
- Optional extras

The number of attendees

As discussed earlier, the most productive CAB meetings have between eight and 16 customer attendees. This creates a balanced discussion with multiple points of view represented. Having fewer than eight creates a conversation lacking depth. If you find yourself with fewer than eight customer attendees, consider delaying the meeting until more customers can confirm their attendance. You'll enjoy a better return on investment. Adding attendees obviously increases the variable costs.

The length and number of CAB meetings per year

The first CAB meeting is usually a ¾-day-long session with a network reception and dinner the evening before. Subsequent CAB meetings may also be ¾ day engagements, or depending on the depth of the agenda, they may extend to a full day or a day and a half. While expanding from a ¾-day to a full day won't usually result in additional hotel or service fees, extending the CAB for *multiple days* will have an impact on your hotel, food, and after-hour expenses. Also, if you hire a professional facilitator, the facilitation fees for a multi-day engagement will likely be a bit higher.

Meeting venue & hotel accommodations

Of course, the hotel rooms and meeting facilities must be of a professional quality and comfort. However, you don't need to break the bank to host the meeting in the best, most expensive hotel available. Customers care more about the agenda than they do the hotel accommodations and meeting rooms. A robust, interactive agenda focused on topics they care about will forgive a less than five-star-quality hotel experience. However, not even the priciest Ritz-Carlton and world-class cuisine will forgive a substandard agenda lacking meaningful content. Hotel and meeting facility prices vary widely, so investigate multiple properties in several cities. Ask for discounts for bundled services.

Professional facilitator

Professional CAB facilitators are experts who know how to design a CAB meeting to address your specific objectives. He or she will focus on the strategy and execution to ensure you exceed the expectations of your executives and your customers. Typical costs for engaging a professional facilitator can range widely per meeting. Expect to pay more for meetings held overseas or if you require additional facilitators to run multiple breakout sessions at the same time. If you plan to hold more than one CAB meeting per year, consider asking the facilitator to bundle his or her services. He or she will likely provide a discount.

Guest speakers

The CAB is not a conference; customers attend the meetings because they want to be part of the discussion. Sitting and listening to talking heads all day isn't what they signed up for. However, as your CAB becomes more established and interactive between the face-to-face meetings, some companies decide to include a guest speaker as an added perk for the CAB members. If the speaker's topic is directly relevant and offers a perspective the customers are not likely to have heard, then it makes good sense. A guest speaker can also be very effective in preparing members for a specific breakout session. For example, the speaker may offer a unique view of industry trends; the customers then partake in a breakout session where they discuss the implications of those trends on their businesses. Fees for hiring a guest speaker will vary. This cost needs to be carefully considered because they will only be presenting for an hour or so, yet you've paid their services for a full day. If possible, negotiate other services into this fee.

Network reception and dinner

Sometimes you can find a hotel with a very good restaurant for these events. Other times you may want to host the reception in a separate location. Either works fine. The most important consideration is to have it hosted in a private room. If you choose a dinner location away from the hotel, transportation cost will be additional. Again, prices will vary.

Production of a CAB welcome package

Plan on distributing a hardcopy or electronic welcome package to customers upon check-in. This is not an expensive item to produce, but it is extremely important for reinforcing the high quality atmosphere of your CAB. The CAB welcome package or booklet is similar to a playbill you would receive when attending the theater. It includes the following information:

- Welcome letter signed by the CEO
- Page with the logos of all attending customers
- Copy of the agenda
- Short biographies and photos of all participants (customers, attending executives, and the facilitator)
- The CAB meeting evaluation form

Customer appreciation gift

"Do we pay customers for attending our CAB?" The answer is no. In fact, if you offer to do so, they may infer that you are trying to bribe them. Their company guidelines, as well as some federal regulations (Sarbanes-Oxley Act of 2002) specify strict rules of corporate behavior. However, it is very appropriate to offer a small gift to show that you have appreciated their time. Regardless what you offer, some attendees may not be able to accept any gift. This is especially true of attendees representing government institutions. The best gifts are the ones that are relevant to the relationship your company has with these customers. Any gift that comes with a monetary designation is not appropriate, so avoid giving gifts such as cash cards, coupons, or credits to your company store. Usually, gifts are under $100 per customer. Here are a few examples of gifts that were appreciated by the customers who received them.

- One company offered logoed shirts, knapsacks, and other gear that customers wore or used during the multi-day meeting.

- A knowledge management company provided all attendees with a high-end flash drive containing an abundance of valuable information, collateral, and reference materials.

- A video streaming company offered customers a small tablet computer preloaded with access to the customer's website so they could see how their content would be displayed on such a device. (This was one of the more expensive gifts offered to customers, but it was relevant to their business and the host company viewed the cost as justifiable.)

Ground transportation

It is customary to pay all fees for ground transportation between the airport and the hotel. The choice of city for hosting the CAB will have an impact on this cost, as you'll pay much more in New York City than you will in San Antonio. Also, if you plan to hold the network reception and dinner at an offsite location, you'll need to arrange shuttles for the group, even if the reception is held only a few blocks a way.

Optional extras

This is completely discretionary. There are no expectations for paying for outside activities. While members of various CABs appreciated a night out at the House of Blues, a round of golf, or a private tour of the Dallas Cowboys Stadium, it was the host company's decision, not a precondition of the CAB, to include them. The selection, if any, is up to you and your management team.

10: GROUND RULES FOR EMPLOYEES

This chapter is short but critically important because inappropriate behaviors can shut down the CAB. Here are five rules to obey. Always.

1. Don't sell

A most awkward moment occurred in London in a global CAB meeting. A customer was answering a question about an industry trend that was affecting his business. He explained that his priorities were shifting and he was rethinking his strategy in favor for a different type of IT infrastructure. It was at this time when an uninvited regional sales manager rudely interrupted with, "You know we make that, don't you?" You could have heard a pin drop. Unfortunately, moments like this are not rare. Another company invited their sales account managers to join the group for the networking reception (they were excluded from the CAB meeting the following day). One of the customers joked with one of the sales reps, "Are you now going to pounce on me to buy something?" Both of these uncomfortable situations can easily be avoided: Don't sell.

2. **Don't answer email, phone calls, or texts at the CAB**

We all know that everyone is busy and multitasking is a standard business practice. But when answering emails, taking calls, or thumbing texts are allowed at the CAB meeting, it is disrespectful and annoying. Also, side conversations in the back of the room between company observers should never be allowed. (Yes, everyone can hear you.) Please wait for the breaks.

3. **No in-and-out privileges**

Customers can't get up and leave, so neither should you. Customers also hate when a CEO joins the meeting in the morning only to say, "Have a great meeting," and then leaves. CAB attendees are executives, too. They've been told the CAB is of strategic importance, and they expect to have a dialog with the executive staff. When the CEO doesn't have the time to participate it sends the wrong message. This is also true for any company executive who wanders in and out. The rule is: If you are at the CAB meeting, you are at the CAB meeting. Stay focused. Be attentive. This may be the most valuable, strategic conversation you have with this important group of customers all year. Treat it as such.

4. **Don't be defensive**

It is not required that CAB participants agree with everything your company does, nor do you need to agree with everything customers say. It's human nature to want to show that you are right, earning endorsements from customers at every turn. But, when customers don't understand your presentation or offer another opinion, your first instinct may be to respond quickly with a "but …. " Some executives, without realizing it, begin to speak faster, louder, or longer, as if the sound of their voice will sway the audience to the his or her point of view. Relax. It's okay. Do not defend. Instead, try to understand where the confusion is or why they don't agree.

5. **You are there to listen**

The agenda, taken as a whole, should allow for customers talking 80% of the time. This means that the host company should be listening 80% of the time. A successful CAB meeting is not about an endless stream of presentations. It's about a dialog with and between CAB members. Listening is not a sign of weakness; it's a sign of strength, empathy, and genuine interest.

11: FREQUENTLY ASKED QUESTIONS

Q1: What is a CAB?
A: Simply put, a CAB is a *strategy-level* focus group – a sounding board for your leadership team to learn from and better understand your most important customers. The CAB is *not* a product focus group, nor is it a sales event. CAB meetings are opportunities to test ideas, preview business plans, and solicit feedback that will guide your company vision and product roadmaps. Taking full advantage of a CAB provides a very effective way to validate that your company vision and product direction are in sync with your customers' business plans and priorities. In addition to meeting face-to-face once or twice a year, CAB members may interact with you to receive interim updates via webinars, conference calls, or through email correspondence throughout the year.

Q2: Why will customers attend my CAB?
A: Senior executives attend CAB meetings for three reasons. First, they rarely have the opportunity to network with their peers to discuss and debate how the world around them affects their businesses. They are eager to explore and compare notes with other executives who are wrestling with

the same business challenges. The second reason is that they want to better understand your vision and business strategy so they can leverage it to their own advantage. And third, they want access to your executive team so they can give you directional guidance and product feedback which will help you help them even more.

Q3: But will these customers want to participate?
A: Yes. For any given CAB, there is always a set of customers who already know each other – either personally, or by reputation. (This tends to be true the higher up you go in the organization.) Because the CAB focuses on business-level issues, not proprietary strategies or customer product plans, these executives will have no trouble sharing their needs, interests, and recommendations to help your company improve or expand the value you are already providing.

Q4: Is it okay to invite customers from the same industry?
A: It depends. Take care not to invite two obvious competing customers from the same industry. For example, inviting an executive from Ford *and* one from GM would not be appropriate. However, the world of hi-tech is filled with "co-opetition" where one day your customers are competitors with each other, the next day they are partners. The lines are less clear here. Let your judgment be your guide.

Q5: Should we mix customers and prospects?
A: Never. Let's be honest: The only reason you'd consider mixing customers and prospects is so that the customers can convince your prospects to buy your products and services. That's a worthy goal, but it doesn't fit the objective of the CAB. CABs require that all attendees have a similar understanding of your products, services, and value

proposition. Without that shared history, prospects cannot provide you with any meaningful guidance. Leave the mixing of customers and prospects to your annual user conference, CIO breakfasts, and tradeshows.

Q6: Should we include partners?
A: No. Adding partners into the mix just creates more confusion because partners are interested in a different set of topics, not the least of which is how they can sell more to these customers. Partners represent a sales channel. Since the CAB is not a sales event, it is not appropriate to include them. To do so will create a layer of awkwardness and possibly even a conflict of interest. Instead, hold a separate Partner Advisory Board (PAB) meeting where the focus can be on how to energize, train, and coach your partners to grow revenue. It is more appropriate to invite them to your annual sales conference.

Q7: What's the ideal size of the CAB?
A: A typical number of total CAB participants in any meeting can range between 20 and 25. That includes the attending customers, your executives, and the facilitator. On average, the most effective CAB meetings have a dozen customer attendees, but the range is usually between eight and 16 customers. One company representative from each customer is invited. Avoid inviting multiple attendees from any single customer; that creates a lopsided discussion. Ideally, the host company will have one executive attending for every two customer attendees; however, you can maintain a 1:1 ratio if politics requires that more of your executives attend. In no case should your executives outnumber the attending customers. Your customers will feel that you are ganging up on them if you do.

Q8: Should I pay customers to attend?
A: No, this is improper etiquette. You want their honest, candid feedback. Any attempt to compensate them will cause them (purposely or unconsciously) to edit their responses to your questions, or worse, provide you with an answer that they think you want to hear, not the one you need to hear.

Q9: What is the term of CAB membership?
A: The term is subjective, although a general guideline suggests 18 – 24 months. We want CAB members to have continuity with the discussions that unfold and build over time. Having said that, it is common for new customers to cycle into each meeting. It is not unusual to have 30-50% turnover because of schedule conflicts. Rather than viewing this as a problem, consider it an opportunity. Cycling in a few new faces every meeting allows you to broaden the CAB base, while tuning the invitation list to meet the specific objective and agenda for each meeting.

Q10: How often should I run CAB meetings?
A: The engagement model for CAB customers can vary greatly. Usually, there is at least one face-to-face meeting per year. Companies that have a lot going on may choose to have a face-to-face meeting twice per year. Some companies also include a quarterly webinar, teleconference, or email to communicate updates between meetings. Some also offer a specific CAB web-portal where members communicate directly with each other as often as they like.

Q11: I'm introducing a new product. How can I get the CAB members to give me relevant feedback on something they haven't seen yet?

A: To get relevant feedback on a new product or service, focus on customer pain points, priorities, and business problems, not on features and benefits. The best approach is to structure an agenda in the following way:

- State a business hypothesis related to a customer problem they are trying to solve, and one that your new product addresses (but don't unveil your new product yet).

- Ask direct questions that engage customers to share their business priorities and criteria for solving these problems.

- Now reveal your new product concept and ask customers to offer feedback as it addresses the hypothesized problem.

Carefully crafting an agenda and directing the conversation in this way leads to some insights and perspectives that would not have been discovered in a more typical product focus-group discussion. By the way, this CAB conversation does not replace the need to conduct focus groups with users.

Q12: What are the benefits of professional facilitator? Can't the CMO or VP of marketing act as the facilitator?
A: Your chief marketing officer or product managers can be excellent facilitators of user group sessions, but when you want to get insight into your customers' business strategies and priorities and how your company can help, investing in a professional facilitator is very appropriate. Here's why:

- Customers sometimes complain that CAB sessions hosted

by a company executive are highly biased as they overtly drive customers to the host's desired conclusion. Using a facilitator can help create a neutral atmosphere and a safe environment for customers to voice their opinions without discomfort or concern of retribution.

- A professional facilitator is experienced in moderating executive-level meetings, inviting participation from all attendees, recognizing body language, and ensuring the agenda stays on topic. This expertise is not always common in even the most senior VPs and most knowledgeable product managers.

- Lastly, it can be very difficult for an executive to lead a balanced discussion and participate in the meeting at the same time. When executives facilitate their own CABs, they can easily miss nuances offered by customers, or they become unintentionally defensive, causing some customers to pull back from the discussion.

Q13: Although we like the CAB format, we're concerned that the meeting will deteriorate into a series of customer complaints. How can we keep the conversation focused on forward thinking topics?
A: This common fear is easily addressed by setting ground rules and expectations for customer interaction that are communicated both during the invitation process and the start of the actual meeting. These rules remind customers that the agenda will focus on trends, drivers, and priorities, while not diving into specific customer issues. Should inappropriate topics arise, the facilitator should acknowledge them by noting the issue on a "parking lot" flipchart and inviting that customer to explore the topic

offline with the appropriate company representative. Then, the facilitator diplomatically refocuses the discussion to keep the meeting on track.

Q14: When should I start planning our CAB?

A: CAB meetings take 12 weeks to plan, on average. Although the timeline can be accelerated, it is best to avoid the temptation of throwing a CAB together quickly. Customers can tell sloppy work. You don't want to risk being unprepared for this meeting. At stake are your reputation and your best customers' loyalty. Additionally, your customers are busy people, just like you. Their calendars are already getting booked for the next quarter. You need to give them plenty of lead-time so they can save the date for you. You'll also benefit from having enough time to interview your customers to tune the agenda through the CAB-preparation process.

Q15: What are the wrong reasons for holding a CAB?

A: CABs with inappropriate objectives end up damaging the host company's relationship with customers. For example, the following objectives are *not* appropriate for a CAB:

- To promote a sales event to drive immediate bookings. *Instead, host a breakfast series with customers and prospects, inviting them to talk about specific applications and use cases for your products and services.*

- To socialize with a large group of customers, and without an agenda. *Instead, add a customer-appreciation day at the end of your annual user conference.*

- To prioritize product features. *Instead, hold a product focus group with users.*

- To publicly launch a new product or service. *Instead, execute an integrated marketing campaign.*

- To discuss customer support issues unique to each customer. *Instead, set up an annual account review meeting.*

Q16: Should we videotape or audiotape our meetings?

A: Absolutely not. When customers know they are being recorded they will be guarded in their answers. They will either self-edit their responses, or they won't talk. No one wants their words used against them. The facilitator will capture notes on flipcharts so everyone can see them. In addition, assign a designated note taker from your organization who is also a subject-matter expert. Their job is not to be a stenographer; no one will ever read 300 pages of verbatim conversations. However, we do want them to capture key comments. After the meeting, the facilitator and designated note taker will compare their notes and produce two final reports: one detailed for internal use only, the other, an executive summary to share with the attending customers.

Q17: What customer communication takes place after the CAB meeting?

A: The most immediate action you should take is to thank the customers for participating. This is usually done with an email sent by the CEO or CAB sponsor within 24 hours of the close of the meeting. Surprisingly, many CAB customers complain that they never receive any acknowledgement or thanks for their contributions. Two to three weeks after the meeting, the host company will offer the attending customers an executive summary report.

Q18: What happens to the data we've now collected?

A: The information, insights, and "aha!" moments experienced in the meeting must be shared internally. The CAB is only a valuable tool to your organization if the results are shared and the team is willing to take action on what they've learned. Because the CAB is a cross-functional initiative, everyone in your company will want to know what happened so they can benefit from the discussions. In addition to creating the CAB Plan-of-Record, some CAB managers present an update at an all-hands meeting, go on an internal company roadshow to visit with teams and share the results, or write an article for the internal newsletter. Not only is it appropriate to share an update of what was discussed, it is very important to talk about any action items and next steps.

Q19: What do you mean, "action items"? Once the meeting is over, aren't we done?

A: Customers want to know that the input they've provided has been useful to your team in some way, even if their feedback leads you *not to* pursue a certain course of action. How was the CAB's input incorporated into your decision-making process? What actions did you take because of the CAB? At the next CAB meeting, the first agenda item will be your giving the customers an update on what you did based on the guidance provided at the last meeting. If you've done nothing, your customers will voice their displeasure. Don't be afraid to communicate what parts of their feedback you considered and what parts were discarded. Tell them why. Be honest with your customers; they want to know what you're thinking. This is part of the collaboration process.

Q20: Are our competitors' holding CAB meetings?
A: The concept of a CAB has grown significantly over the past five years. Google the topic and you can now find a lot of material from practitioners and corporate executives eager to share their best practices. The smart companies are the ones keeping the conversation going with their customers long after the sale has been closed. They have added a CAB in their voice-of-the-customer toolbox. So, are your competitors already holding CABs? It's best to assume they are.

Q21: Where can I get more information on CABs?
A: To learn more about how CABs map to your annual planning process, see *The Flipchart Guide™ to Customer Advisory Boards, Volume 1: Is your company ready?*

You can find more information on CAB best practices, case studies, example agendas, and a variety of other relevant information on the Customer Advisory Board blog:

Your CAB resource center
http://customeradvisoryboards.wordpress.com

ABOUT THE AUTHOR

J. Michael (Mike) Gospe, Jr. is an accomplished leader, marketing strategist, and corporate executive who understands what it takes to market and sell to today's business-to-business companies. His expertise is in integrated marketing and "voice of the customer" (VOC) programs, including designing and facilitating Customer Advisory Board (CAB) meetings and executive planning sessions. Mike is co-founder and principal of KickStart Alliance (**www.kickstartall.com**), a sales and marketing leadership consulting team, where he leads the marketing operations and CAB practices. Mike also conducts team-based marketing workshops on building personas, crafting differentiating positioning statements, and drafting customer-ready messaging. His fun, practical approach and roll-up-his-sleeves attitude energizes teams, helping them get "real work done," while guiding them to the next level of marketing excellence.

Mike has authored a number of marketing- and sales-related articles, and is a frequent guest speaker at companies, marketing associations, and university business schools. His books, *Marketing Campaign Development: What executives need to know about architecting global integrated marketing campaigns* (2008), *The Marketing High Ground: The essential playbook for B2B marketing practitioners everywhere* (2011), and the new *The Marketing High Ground series* (2012) are available in paperback and for the Kindle.

Join Mike on **LinkedIn: www.linkedin.com/in/mikegospe**

Follow Mike on **Twitter: www.twitter.com/mikegospe**

OTHER WORKS

Marketing Campaign Development: What executives need to know about architecting global integrated marketing campaigns (2008) discusses the two most fundamental questions marketers are asked:

1. *How do I determine the optimum marketing communications mix?*

2. *How do I best manage internal politics to launch my marketing campaign and nurture it for best results?*

Written for marketing leaders at every level, this book answers these two key questions by taking you step-by-step through the disciplined, yet practical, process of designing truly integrated marketing communications plans that work. In these pages, you'll find a prescription for building a successful, repeatable campaign-development process, including the necessary templates and helpful, practical tips and techniques required for success. The process and best practices revealed in this book have been used at Adobe, Aspect, Cisco, Genesys, HP, Informatica,  Sun, Symantec, and many other companies, large and small. You will learn the secrets for optimizing lead generation programs and achieving an even greater return on your marketing investment.

You can also find more marketing best-practices information, tips, templates, and techniques at:

http://marketingcampaigndevelopment.wordpress.com

The Marketing High Ground: The essential playbook for B2B marketing practitioners everywhere (2011) explores the following three best practices:

1. Personas: *how to craft a targeted persona as a reflection of a real target market*
2. Positioning statements: *how to draft compelling positioning statements that are truly unique when compared against competitive alternatives*
3. Messaging: *how to tell your story through a well-honed set of relevant messages guaranteed to engage the persona and not waste their time*

Packed with practical and powerful advice, templates, and techniques, this playbook is a valuable resource that guides marketers to dramatically improve their go-to-market programs and drive revenue. There are a lot of marketing books out there that talk a good story. This one actually shows marketers how to make a real difference. This action-oriented show-and-tell book focuses on how to build and execute more effective integrated marketing campaigns. These three best practices will put you in tune with your customers' buying process. This book shows you how, with lots of examples, descriptions, and a prescription for success. Whether you work at a large enterprise, a start-up company, or a family run business, these best practices are essential for driving successful product launches and executing integrated marketing campaigns that drive sales.

You can also find more tips, and techniques at:

http://marketinghighground.wordpress.com

Made in the USA
San Bernardino, CA
16 June 2016